# Three Steps to
# SMALL BUSINESS SUCCESS

DICK B MILLER

*outskirts press*

Three Steps to Small Business Success
All Rights Reserved.
Copyright © 2019 Dick B Miller
v2.0

The opinions expressed in this manuscript are solely the opinions of the author and do not represent the opinions or thoughts of the publisher. The author has represented and warranted full ownership and/or legal right to publish all the materials in this book.

This book may not be reproduced, transmitted, or stored in whole or in part by any means, including graphic, electronic, or mechanical without the express written consent of the publisher except in the case of brief quotations embodied in critical articles and reviews.

Outskirts Press, Inc.
http://www.outskirtspress.com

ISBN: 978-1-9772-1084-5

Cover Photo © 2019 www.gettyimages.com. All rights reserved - used with permission.

Outskirts Press and the "OP" logo are trademarks belonging to Outskirts Press, Inc.

PRINTED IN THE UNITED STATES OF AMERICA

# Table of Contents

**Introduction** — i

**Step One: Make a Plan** — 1
  Tips for Effective Writing. .. .. .. .. .. .. .. .. .. .. .. .. 6

**Step Two: Lead the Way** — 9

**Step Three: Share the Profit** — 21

**Other Considerations** — 31
  The Importance of Writing .. .. .. .. .. .. .. .. .. .. .. 31
  Dealing with Change.. .. .. .. .. .. .. .. .. .. .. .. .. .. 33
  Keeping it Simple.. .. .. .. .. .. .. .. .. .. .. .. .. .. .. 34
  Decisions .. .. .. .. .. .. .. .. .. .. .. .. .. .. .. .. .. .. 37
  Contracts and Agreements .. .. .. .. .. .. .. .. .. .. 38
  Hiring Employees . .. .. .. .. .. .. .. .. .. .. .. .. .. .. 41

**Appendix and Additional Resources** — 47
  Business Planning Guide .. .. .. .. .. .. .. .. .. .. .. 49
  Job Description Format .. .. .. .. .. .. .. .. .. .. .. 52
  The Small Business Checkup. .. .. .. .. .. .. .. .. 54
  Creating a Company Newsletter .. .. .. .. .. .. .. 56
  Sample Profit Sharing Program .. .. .. .. .. .. .. 57
  Developing a Financial Projection.. .. .. .. .. .. .. 60
  The B Corporation Concept .. .. .. .. .. .. .. .. .. 63

# Introduction

Starting and operating a small business is the subject of this book. While there are many books on this topic, most, in my opinion, are too detailed and complex to be immediately useful. My plan was to write a simple, clear, and easy to understand guide that, like a well written business plan, will be an enduring reference and source of guidance.

Small businesses in America are a dynamic, major part of our economy. They account for about 50% of our gross domestic product (GDP is the total goods and services produced by all entities), there are about 23 million small businesses in the United States and they employ about half of all workers in the country. Most small businesses are home based. According to the U.S. Small Business Administration, over 500,000 new small businesses start up each year and they account for 75% of all new jobs created.

But the failure rate is high. After four years, about half of all startups are gone. If this failure rate can be reduced, even by a small fraction, the economic benefits will be significant. My hope is that this book and the guidance it provides will move us in that direction.

# Three Steps to Small Business Success

1. Make a Plan
2. Lead the Way
3. Share the Profit

# STEP ONE

## Make a Plan

*Overview* A written business plan is your first step toward success. It is a tedious process but well worth the effort. A good business plan touches all aspects of any business – marketing, finance, management, operations and other, often unique considerations. The time and energy required to write a business plan will yield a detailed knowledge and understanding of these business elements, forming a strong foundation on which to build and grow the business. It is also a great way to inform others – lenders, investors, employees, suppliers – about the business. Getting help to write a business plan can save time, but the business owner should be intimately involved to get the most benefit from the process. Once written, the plan should be periodically reviewed to see how it compares to actual performance. This practice will reveal opportunities for updating the plan, making it more accurate, precise and useful over time. Remember the old adage that failure to plan is a plan to fail.

*Do the Research* By definition, a business plan is forward looking, a projection of the future, a goal setting process, a roadmap of how to get from here to there, and a guideline for achieving business goals. It specifies what resources will be needed and establishes time lines and milestones. So, before writing, some research is required. Devote a certain amount of time focused exclusively on gathering information. Don't try to analyze or review this information, just collect it for later review. Take notes at all your meetings, find relevant publications and industry information and standards, make a list of important contacts, record key numbers and statistics, clip and save newspaper and magazine articles, gather educational transcripts and licenses, identify regulations and regulatory contacts, create spreadsheets and so on. Put all this information in one big box and keep it handy as you begin writing the plan.

Consider how David Brooks does his writing. Brooks is a columnist at the *New York Times*, an author, national speaker and frequent guest commentator on National Public Radio and Television. He begins by collecting information in several folders with labels reflecting his various interests. When it comes time to write, he spreads this collection in a circle on his living room floor, sits in the middle of it and begins organizing and sorting through the material. He makes notes while doing this, which function as the beginning of an outline for use later as he starts writing his next commentary.

To get you started, here is a list of research topics that affect most businesses in one way or another. You can use this list to label files, envelopes or electronic folders in which to collect your research information.

- Market Opportunity – Pinpoint, verify and quantify the market opportunity. This is the first and most important

piece of research information because everything else will be based on it.
- Competitive Environment – Identify, list and evaluate competitors and the environment in which they operate. This will help you understand the playing field, the niche you will want to occupy and how aggressive you must be to compete.
- Industry Trends – Study the industry and examine trends. Every industry is changing, some more rapidly than others. Change provides opportunity, so knowing what's happening in the industry can reveal gaps and openings.
- Publications – Get your hands on publications from trade groups, regulators and industry associations. This is a reliable way to become informed about the latest developments in almost any industry. Look for local, state and national chapters and groups.
- Suppliers – List and evaluate suppliers, vendors, contractors and others who serve the industry, especially locally. These businesses and organizations should welcome your questions because you represent a potential new customer.

*Use a Planning Outline* After you've spent adequate time gathering research information, you're ready to begin writing your business plan. A planning outline is a useful tool for this because it poses questions and guides the writer as the plan is developed. A one-page Business Planning Outline is included in the appendix of this book. The outline has eight sections:

- Summary – This is a brief, one page overview of the business. Sometimes it is called the executive summary.

- The Business and the Industry – In more detail, this part is a summary of the business, the industry in which it operates, important market and operational considerations, requirements, regulations, constraints and resources.
- Marketing Plan – The heart of the business plan comes next in the form of five major categories. Marketing is the first of these because everything else is based on the market. What's most important is to clearly identify, verify and quantify the market in which the business will operate.
- Financial Plan – A financial plan is a quantitative outlook of how the business is expected to perform. This financial plan is an essential tool for comparing actual with planned outcomes.
- Operations Plan – This section of the business plan describes how the business will function – its manufacturing or service delivery process.
- Management Plan – Here is an explanation of how the enterprise will be run, by whom and with what methods and techniques. A management philosophy should be included, reflecting the attitude and approach of the owner.
- Other Considerations – Because every business is unique, there will always be distinctive aspects to consider. For example, transportation and support requirements of a particular location, weather and climate, financial sources, personal experience, succession considerations, relations with relatives and investors, timing, licensing, regulatory restraints, emerging opportunities, and so on.

- Supporting Documents – This is a list of the details behind the business plan. It would include things such as market research facts and findings, competitive analysis, statistical data, historical trends, consulting reports, operational details, flow charts, and similar types of information.

*Write the Plan* Now comes the nitty gritty of actually putting the plan on paper. One of the questions that arises about a business plan is how detailed should it be? The best answer is to make the business plan comprehensive and concise, a tall order and a writing challenge. To be useful, a well written business plan must be comprehensive, that is, it includes all the important aspects of operating the business. Many of the minor details can be omitted from the main body of the plan but not the major ones. In addition, documents and information that supplement the plan in more detail can be listed and included among the supporting documents. To be both comprehensive and concise requires skill in summarizing, giving the big picture with the fewest possible words. To this end, I suggest using a progressive, three-step approach to writing as follows:

> Make an Outline – Step one is to create an outline using the eight sections of the planning guide. In each section, write key words and phrases that come to mind, major points and conclusions from market research, essential facts, quantities, statistics and elements. Focus on an outline, not on writing full sentences.
>
> Write a Rough Draft – Step two is to write a rough draft based on the outline. A good way to do this is to write fast when the ideas flow, to get thoughts down

on paper without regard to grammar, spelling, word choice or sentence structure. Rewriting later will improve the writing, making it more accurate, clear and concise.

Polish the Rough Draft – Lastly, polish the writing with a focus on clarity and brevity. Carefully review and correct spelling and grammar, restructure sentences and paragraphs, consider word choice, eliminate duplications and redundancies.

## Tips for Effective Writing

- Write in short, simple sentences; avoid compound sentences
- Use simple words
- Avoid jargon, cliché, and slang
- Use action verbs
- Avoid acronyms and abbreviations
- Use present tense

*Keep It Brief* How long should a good business plan be? As short as possible. This is the correct answer because a good business plan is one that is periodically reviewed. This "as short as possible" requirement means 12 to 15 pages tops. A 50 or 75-page business plan may be a literary masterpiece but its length and complexity are daunting for a small business owner. Such a plan will just sit on the shelf or in the file cabinet and seldom if ever actually be used; the effort to review all those pages is just too great. This is not to say that details are ignored; however, they should be kept in supplemental files, spreadsheets, binders and books -- not included in the business plan itself. The business plan should include only a brief reference and a list of these supporting documents.

*Be Future Oriented* Remember that a business plan is forward looking. It is written to describe what the owner intends to make happen over a future period. For example, the financial plan should project revenue and expense for five or more years. Other parts of the plan will reflect this projection and period of time. As the business expands, additional equipment and supplies will be needed, a larger operating space required and additional people hired to handle the work load. Hopefully, the business owner will be faced with challenges related to growth, the best kind to have. New small businesses either grow or shrink, but few remain static; sadly, many fail.

*Know When to Call it Done* One of the final challenges to writing a business plan is knowing when to stop. In a way, writing a plan is like painting a beautiful landscape. The painter can continue making small changes and additions but eventually must stop so the painting can be offered for sale, a final masterpiece. Likewise, a business owner must stop writing and get on with launching the business. Exactly when this occurs is unpredictable and situational, of course, but here are some guidelines to help you know when to call the plan done.

- First, realize that there is no such thing as a perfect business plan, just as there is no such thing as a perfect painting. Some are better than others but none are perfect.
- Next, set a time limit for planning before the process begins. A time limit should be flexible to allow for

uncertainties, but having a proposed time allocation for doing research and another for writing the plan can be helpful.
- Before moving forward with your plan, have it reviewed by outside specialists or professionals. Input from a Certified Public Accountant, a small business broker, a lender, an insurance agent, a trade group representative, a supplier, or a college professor can be enlightening. Seek critical review, not complimentary agreement. Ask for suggestions and vital questions. Be prepared to be surprised.
- Last, make final adjustments to the plan, put it on the shelf and move on. Call it good – for now – because it is the best you can do given the time and resources available. You may need to review or use parts of the plan or the supporting documents to begin implementation, but it should not be necessary to review the plan very often. Because you have been directly and intimately involved in writing the plan, you know it well enough to go ahead and start running the business. Be sure, however, to schedule quarterly reviews of the plan.

# STEP TWO

## Lead the Way

*Overview* After the business plan is written, the owner must begin implementing it. This is often a solo effort which can continue for a considerable time before others are involved. For example, someone who starts a home service business like window washing, carpet cleaning or landscape maintenance may operate alone for a year or two until the client base grows enough to justify hiring the first employee.

Even though the business has no employees for the first few years, leadership is still required. Think of the people that a small business owner deals with even before hiring employees: suppliers, equipment dealers, maintenance workers, regulators, accountants, and most importantly, customers and their family, neighbors and friends. The business owner must interact successfully with all these people if he or she is to succeed.

So, in addition to performing the work of the business, that is, cleaning windows or installing carpet or mowing lawns, the owner is required to establish and maintain positive relationships with a diverse group of people. It's not surprising that many small businesses either don't grow or fail under these demands, as it's common for owners to underestimate them. The business plan should reflect these demands and how to deal with them. Knowing how to influence others in a positive way is an essential skill for business owners, and understanding leadership is the key.

*Build Leadership Skill* A new business owner is not necessarily an effective leader. Leadership is a skill that must be learned and strengthened through practice. Prior experience in a leadership position is helpful but not essential. Most of the skills involved can be learned quickly with the right attitude and preparation. The definition of leadership includes statements like:

- To guide or direct in a course of action
- To show the way by going in advance
- To direct the performance and activities of others

A leader is one who has authority and responsibility over others. This mainly refers to employees but also vendors, suppliers, contractors, regulators and others who supply and support the business. In all cases, the business leader should seek to establish smooth working relationships with everyone involved in or with the business. Here are some tried and true techniques for effective business leadership.

*Set the Leadership Style* There are many styles of leadership. For example, military leadership is the most rigid, requiring unquestioned compliance with orders. In similar fashion in the business world, an autocratic leader directly oversees most activities and employees have little or nothing to say or contribute. By contrast, in organizations with well-trained and experienced employees, a leader may provide only general guidance, then allow workers to continue fairly autonomously. Participative leadership encourages teamwork, input and shared involvement in decision-making. An inspiring leader promotes a vision of the future with energy and passion. Operating a small business offers unlimited potential to set your particular leadership style reflecting your personality, your commitment, and your experience. This offers a satisfying opportunity to be inspiring, visionary, energetic, passionate, and even transformational.

*Describe Your Business Ethic* Having a written business ethic or code of conduct is a helpful leadership tool and a way to describe how you plan to manage your business. It is a wonderful opportunity to be creative, to express your personal attitudes, behaviors and character. You may want to include this description in the Management Plan section of the business plan or utilize it as a supporting document. Either way, a written business ethic helps maintain consistency in your approach to leadership and demonstrates that you have thoughtfully developed a standard for behavior in your business. A business ethic should be inclusive. That is, it should clearly cover all business activities by everyone in the business. It describes the culture, the values, the attitude, the "way we do things in this business." Here is an example of such a business ethic:

> Teamwork – In this business, we work together in various groups. We join with others in our work on a regular basis. We encourage others to join us and share ideas and experience. We share information openly. We

keep team members informed. We conduct brief and focused meetings.

Fair Play – We treat everyone the same. We do not do special favors or make conflicting deals. Agreements are in writing and we do not enter verbal contracts. We do not ask or offer to share revenue with vendors, suppliers, clients or customers.

Open Mindedness – We seek change. We constantly search for ways to improve. Our minds are open to new ideas and suggestions. We seek feedback. We encourage independent and critical thinking. We measure performance. We report regularly.

*Use the Management Cycle* Most business activity falls into repetitive cycles. For example, customers purchase a product or service, the money from the sale goes into the business deposit account, a record of the transaction is created, a thank you note goes out to the customer who contacts the business for more products or services in the future and the cycle is repeated. There are many overlapping and interrelated cycles like this in every business. Think of the various raw materials coming into a small cabinet manufacturing business. These materials are turned into finished products and delivered to a remodeling or construction site and the manufacturer is paid when the cabinets are installed and the customer is satisfied. Along the way, multiple entities and processes are involved, the lumber yard, those who built the cabinets, the installer, the business's accounting system, state and federal authorities who collect taxes and fees and on and on. Cycles are important because they establish predictable and reliable ways to operate and help assure the correct outcome.

Fortunately, there is a simple and reliable cycle for managing a small business, a tried and true method that many managers use. It is based on four fundamental management functions: planning, organizing, leading and controlling. Graphically, a circle represents this management cycle quite well. The circle shows a continuing, repetitive process that always starts – and ends – with planning. Although there are four management functions, they do not always occur in a direct sequence as the circle indicates. At any given time, a manager can be performing one function, then quickly jump to another as the situation requires. For example, a manager may be spending time with a vendor arranging a delivery schedule (organizing) when a call comes in about an accounting question (controlling).

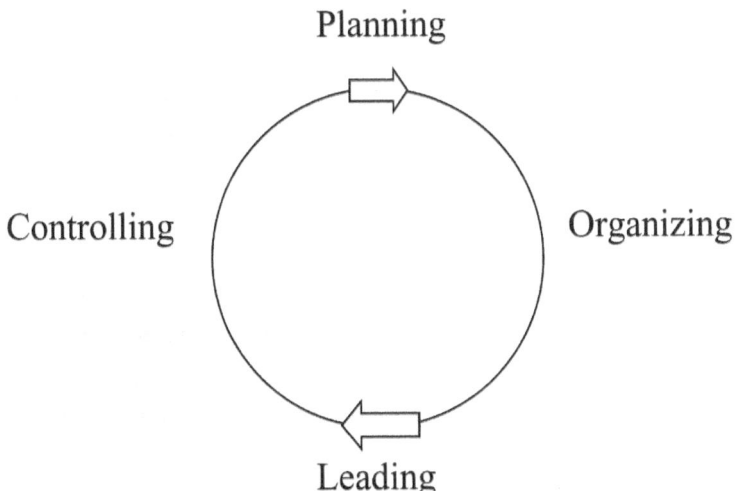

A manager must be flexible and patient to move from one function to another as needed. On the other hand, the management cycle is an overall, systematic sequence to guide a small business owner. Here is a brief description of the four functions of management in the cycle.

Planning – Always have a plan before acting. Some plans are short-term, others intermediate or long-term, special purpose, single use and so on. Oftentimes, in small business, a plan ends up being a process, such as a manufacturing schedule or a routine schedule for maintenance. Essentially, these are plans that have become procedures, but they are still plans. Because no plan is perfect, adjustments are inevitable, needed, even desired and expected. A plan should be adjusted based on results and outcomes in relation to goals and expectations. This requires that quantitative goals be included in the plan. For a small business manager, this is a tall order and one of the most demanding tasks. In the day-to-day hustle, it is difficult to find time to plan. The best way to overcome this difficulty is to carefully schedule a period for planning, an afternoon, a weekend day or another period that is set aside just for planning.

Organizing – In a nutshell, organizing is identifying the necessary resources and putting them in place. It means getting things in order and ready to operate, establishing controls and schedules, listing necessary quantities and materials, arranging for purchase and delivery, contacting vendors and suppliers to establish routines and schedules, selecting and training employees. For example, before you hire your first employee, it's wise to develop a job description and a pay scale and know what the tax implications of hiring will be. The job description should be no more than one page, a condensed, summarized explanation of the work to be performed and the skills, abilities, training, knowledge and experience required. Moreover, a job description is a useful tool for interviewing because it helps keep the focus on the job opportunity in relation to a job applicant. A format for a job description is included in the appendix.

Leading – Back, once again to leading and leadership. Once you have a written business plan in place and finished organizing to begin operation, it's time to take the lead. This means being an enthusiastic guide to others even before hiring the first employees. Remember that the business leader should seek to establish smooth working relationships with everyone involved in or with the business, not just employees. However, hiring the first employees requires additional leadership skill, a more demanding and focused effort. The preferred approach is to consider each new employee a permanent, long-term member of the business team and to instill this attitude in each new hire. This approach pays off, even with part time and seasonal employees. Here are some tips on leading and encouraging new employees:

- Create a work environment that is comfortable and secure, where employees can focus on their work, knowing they are in a stable, reliable job, valued by their employer, and a vital member of your team.
- Be an enthusiastic teacher, mentor, and coach. Encourage, reward and praise quality work, give regular feedback both verbally and in writing. A hand-written note of appreciation from the boss is a powerful motivator.
- Provide quality training. Many technical jobs require licensure and certification and offer progressive levels

of qualification. Encourage employees to pursue these goals and reward and acknowledge them for succeeding. Each training achievement should be viewed as a success for the entire team and the business.

- Encourage initiative. Employees should feel encouraged to learn their jobs well. This requires some type of regular communication between supervisor and employee such as a monthly review of activities. This can be informal, for example, taking a few minutes at the beginning of a new month to talk things over. It provides an opportunity for feedback to the employee on job performance and to pass along other information such as a printed report of activity, comments from customers, technical and safety bulletins and so on. Encouraging initiative should be a two-way effort in which the employee feels comfortable and secure in giving feedback about the job and its challenges. For the supervisor or manager, this is an opportunity to provide encouragement, pointing out and showing ways to improve efficiency and gain skill in the job. It is important to remember that not all employees are interested in moving up and taking on more responsibility. Most people just want a steady job, a good work environment and a regular paycheck. Regardless of aspirations and motives, all employees should feel encouraged to perform well and master their current jobs.
- Give authority in proportion to responsibility. If employees are expected to be responsible for their decisions and actions, they must be granted the authority to make them. To strike the correct balance between authority and responsibility, begin with the responsibilities, then determine what authority is necessary. For example,

an employee who is required to maintain carpet cleaning equipment used each day should be authorized to perform regular maintenance, take the necessary time to do it, purchase needed parts and supplies and learn how to use the equipment efficiently. In another example, an employee who is responsible for scheduling work for a landscape maintenance crew should be authorized to make commitments to customers, select the right crew members, confirm appointments and so on.
- Review the job description. Do this at least once a year with the incumbent in the job. Spend some time discussing the job description and seek to make it accurate and understandable. Employees will know what changes should be made and will feel encouraged by being invited to participate in this process.
- Lead by example. Get your hands dirty to show respect and importance for quality work. When the boss shows how the work is done, it establishes a standard for quality and sets a performance expectation. It is a powerful motivator that reinforces the importance of teamwork.
- Take responsibility when mistakes are made. Employees work for you and ultimately, their mistakes are your responsibility. So, be quick to assume responsibility and shield employees from blame.

Controlling – This final function completes the management cycle. Controlling implies measurement, that is, quantification, numbers, reports, statements and lists. Some are standard reports such as the income statement and the balance sheet, two important financial reports that managers must use and understand. Various other reports will depend on the type of business. For example, in a window cleaning business, the owner will want to know how many customers were served during a particular period, the average revenue from these services, what supplies and materials were used, the labor and transportation costs, etc. Controlling can be thought of as a funnel which brings together important facts about what transpired during a business cycle. After all the planning, organizing and leading, the controlling function is the feedback loop, the details and reports that tell the business owner and managers precisely what happened. This information is vital to continuing the business cycle's next function: planning. Here are some tips on creating a useful system of controls for any business:

- Design and obtain regular reports that relate to goals and budgets set in the business plan. The goals and budgets are the standards against which to measure performance. When examining the income statement and balance sheet, a manager should look for variances or differences from these standards. If planning is meticulous and well executed, the actual performance will be close to the projected numbers. For example, if total income is projected to be $5,000 for the month, the actual income should be between $4,500 and $5,500 which is an acceptable 20% margin of error. In another example, if the number of window washing clients projected for the month of June is 50, the actual number of clients should fall between 40 and 60, also an acceptable margin of 20%. In short, a business owner will use a variety of reports, especially standard reports like the income statement and the balance sheet to monitor performance. Getting to know the numbers in these

and other reports is an essential component of this management function known as controlling.
- Share information in reports with others who should or need to know. The best way to understand and improve the controlling function is to get others involved. Discuss the reports with experts to help make sure you are gleaning the right information. Get answers to questions to clarify your understanding of the reports and be sure to take notes for future use when examining them. Share key information in reports with employees to let them know what they have helped accomplish. Ask for their feedback and opinion on reports so they become part of the process, not just recipients of information.
- Search controls for ways to improve, gain efficiencies, and grasp opportunities. After all, the purpose of this fourth management function – controlling – is to find ways to make positive changes in the business. And, while it is tedious and time consuming, a conscientious manager will carefully examine reports, statistics, facts, figures, numbers and documents, discuss this information with others, and regularly seek opinions, suggestions and ideas. This is a reliable and proven method. With practice, it can – and should – become an everyday practice, part of your attitude and behavior.
- Stay current with industry trends, new technology and the competitive environment. This is crucial because every business and every industry is dynamic and there is no such thing as the status quo. Keeping up with changes is essential to maintain your competitive edge. You can do this by joining a trade association, reading the journals or newsletters made available to

members, being involved in local associations and activities and most importantly, paying attention to what competitors are doing. Watch their advertising, collect their promotional and sales literature, ask employees to add information and be alert to changes.

# STEP THREE

## Share the Profit

*Overview* Net profit is a financial imperative. Although most new small businesses are not profitable for months or even years after startup, they all must eventually become profitable; there is no alternative. The definition of net profit is the money left over after all costs are paid, all salaries and wages, all supplies, services, rent, fuel, utilities, taxes and all other expenses of running the business. There are many reasons why net profit is so critical.

*Why Net Profit is Important* Net profit is an indicator of success in business. It shows that operations are in proper balance. For example, consider how to set the price of your product or service. For net profit to occur from your sales, the price must reflect all operating costs plus a margin for profit. So, if the operating cost is, say, $100 per hour, the price for it should be about $120 per hour. That's a 20% profit margin and an appropriate target for small business. This target profit margin should be explained in the Financial Plan section of the business plan as a stated goal of the business and specifically included in the projected financial statements. While it may not be possible to achieve a 20% profit margin during the start-up phase, it should be later. Net profit is a powerful tool for managing a business because it useful in so many ways. Here are some examples:

- Net profit builds confidence. It indicates success and reflects good management, good planning, good execution, good results.
- Net profit provides flexibility. It opens doors to options and gives the business owner alternatives otherwise not available. How to spend and invest net profit is a wonderful challenge.
- Net profit is a buffer against the unknown and surprises.
- Net profit sharing is a powerful motivator for employees.
- Net profit can be used to stimulate loyalty and respect from outsiders such as vendors, suppliers, contractors and others connected to the business.
- Finally, net profit determines the value of a business.

*Net Profit Builds Confidence* Planning for and achieving net profit is a sure-fire way to confirm and validate the business. It reflects good planning and management and can be used in many ways to enhance the business. Moreover, consistent net profit from one period to another, from one quarter or one year to another builds a solid financial history for the business. This, in turn, motivates talented and skilled employees to stay, is appealing to top job applicants, solidifies relationships with vendors and suppliers, gets the attention of lenders and investors, gives competitive advantage and increases the value of the business.

*Net Profit Provides Flexibility* Think of net profit as a catalyst. It makes many things possible and available. For example, it allows a business to keep pace with changes in technology such as updating a computer system with new hardware and software. It can be used to enter new markets and expand existing ones. In short, it opens doors of opportunity that require some cash to enter. Net profit is the key.

*Net Profit is a Buffer Against the Unknown* In business, as in life, surprises are inevitable. Good planning helps assure that big surprises are anticipated and can be avoided, leaving only small ones to deal with. The saying goes, "Don't sweat the small stuff." Nevertheless, the business owner must still deal with the small surprises and other unknown events and conditions that will inevitably come along. Net profit helps in this effort by providing a cash cushion. Surprises usually involve an unanticipated expense. For example, the state department of employment may decide to increase the cost of unemployment insurance, a fee that every employer must pay in full. Or, a supplier raises the price of imported hinges for cabinet doors on kitchen cabinets that you fabricate. The cost of these surprises is immediate, so having the cash available to pay it becomes an urgent need. Some surprises may even be big enough to require the business to borrow money. The best approach to covering the cost of surprises and the unknown is to set aside some of the net profit in a money market account or business savings account where it is instantly available for use.

*Profit Sharing with Employees* Upon becoming an employer, a small business owner assumes significant new responsibilities. These include training, mentoring, guiding, helping and encouraging new members of the business team. And they must be paid, on time and accurately according to company policy and practice. From this compensation, certain taxes must be withheld and forwarded and other taxes and fees paid in full by the employer, on time and accurately according to government and agency policy and practice, significant responsibilities that carry additional record keeping and reporting requirements. These obligations are peripheral to the real relationship one should establish with all employees. They are members of your team sharing a common effort, a common goal and a common code of business ethics. As leader, the business owner should emphasize and enhance this relationship. One of the most powerful enhancements is sharing net profit. There are several ways to do this, but one simple method is to use a point system. Each employee gets one point for each $100 of annual compensation plus ten points for each six months of employment. Add up all the points and divide it into the profit-sharing allocation. This practice acknowledges that each member of the team has helped create net profit and each should benefit from it in a significant way. Profit sharing connects everyone in the business, confirms their position on the team and motivates them to continue performing well, a potent stimulus. Employees begin to understand that their day-to-day performance makes a real and measurable difference. They are motivated to watch expenses more carefully, look for ways to improve efficiencies and to understand the importance of teamwork in the business.

*Net Profit Stimulates Loyalty and Respect* In addition to enhancing the relationship with employees, net profit can be used to stimulate loyalty and respect among those outside the business, vendors, suppliers, contractors, customers and the public. There are numerous ways to do this from thank you notes to gift certificates to sporting event tickets to golf passes. Some businesses invite customers and vendors to periodic celebrations including food and entertainment. Others award prizes and certificates of recognition. The idea is to acknowledge and confirm the significance of these individuals and groups to the business, and most importantly, to encourage personal relationships. Someone in the business has had a personal interaction with outsiders. For example, a salesperson knows and communicates regularly with a group of customers, an installer has regular dealings with a supplier and sub-contractors, a bookkeeper communicates with a Certified Public Accountant at least once each year. Make the most of these personal relationships by giving team members a little money from net profit. Let them decide how best to use it. In the budget, set aside a small portion of net profit for printed materials such as official thank you notes with the business logo, gift certificates from a favorite restaurant, tickets to the local university's football games and invitations to public events, the list is endless.

*Net Profit Determines Value* Ultimately, a business owner must consider how to leave the business, when to retire or when to sell. After years of building the business and creating value, the time will come – and should be planned – when the owner wants out. Net profit plays a key role in this decision. Here's why. Net profit is the most significant factor in determining the value of a small business. That is, a business that has consistently and increasingly created net profit is worth an amount related to this net profit. Any of several ways to determine the market value of a business all use net profit as a major factor. There are other factors, including the level of sales, the competitive position and prospects for improving it, the growth of market share over time, and the consistency of management and industry trends. However, none is more significant than the net profit the business has consistently produced. A typical calculation of the value of a business is to take the net profit amount and multiply it by a factor of two, three or four to determine the value of a business. For example, if your small business has consistently produced a net profit and the average net profit for the past four years is $100,000 per year, the business will be worth between $200,000 and $400,000. Experts in the field of business valuation have complex formulas, but all are based on this simple, fundamental relationship between net profit and value. No other factors relating to the value of a business come close to the significance of this relationship.

*Net Profit Distribution* To better understand how net profit can be used, consider this breakdown and pie chart showing how net profit is distributed in a sample company with $45,000 in net profit. The business owner has the pleasure of determining how this cash will be used to improve the business.

| Profit Distribution Sample Company with $45,000 net profit | | |
|---|---|---|
| | $ | % |
| Profit Sharing | 22,500 | 50% |
| Management Bonuses | 9,000 | 20% |
| Retained Earnings | 6,750 | 15% |
| Equipment Upgrades | 4,500 | 10% |
| Other Uses | 2,250 | 5% |
| Totals | 45,000 | 100% |

This chart includes five categories. Here are these categories described in more detail:

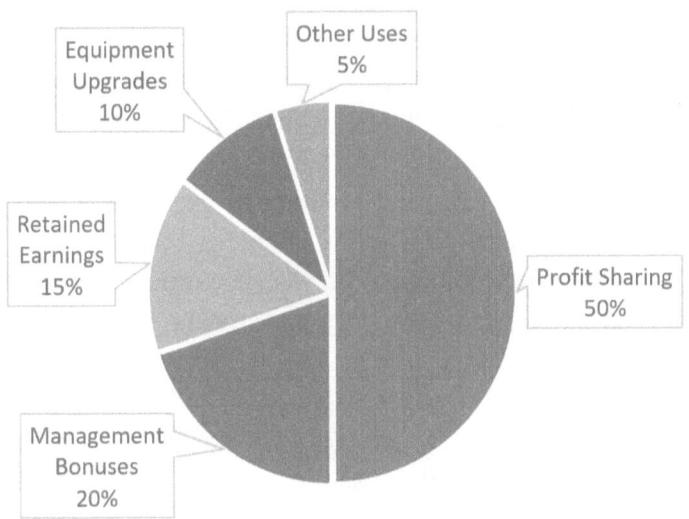

- Profit Sharing – This takes half of net profit, the biggest share. This cash distribution can be considered an incentive and a reward for each employee's contribution. One of the key aspects of profit sharing is that everyone participates on a publicized equitable basis.
- Management Bonuses – In addition to profit sharing, managers can receive an additional bonus. The amount each manager receives can vary but the basis of the variation should be well understood by all managers and should be equitable, that is, even handed and fair. Some considerations for management bonuses include longevity with the company, title and responsibilities, employment contract requirements and performance rating.

- Retained Earnings – Maintaining a cash reserve in small business is a good idea. This balance sheet account should be considered "free" cash. That is, cash on hand for immediate use but without any assigned or pre-determined uses. The cash acts as a buffer against the unknown, a rainy-day fund, a backup cash account. As the fund grows over time, it can be redistributed for special needs such as new equipment, software or any other worthy need.
- Equipment Upgrade – Although upgrades should be worked into each year's operating budget, there are always new items on the wish list in our fast-changing technological world. Upgrades can be made from net profit but should be limited to special needs and desires and not routine upgrades.
- Other Uses – This category can include any number of separate uses such as employee recognition and awards, anniversary celebrations, vendor gifts, facility upgrades and improvements, consultation fees and so on.

*Understanding Cash and Cash Flow* We all know what cash is. It's money in the bank, in your pocket, in your savings account, equity in your home and investments. In a small business, cash moves around in a way that is remarkably similar to the way blood moves through the body. Consider that the flow of blood in our bodies is essential to life. It sustains us by carrying nutrients and oxygen to every part, removing waste byproducts and providing defensive protection against infection and disease. If blood runs out of our body from a severe injury, we soon die.

In a similar way, cash is essential to the life of any business. To begin with, cash comes into a business from the sale of goods or services. It moves from a customer making a payment to a deposit into your bank account. From there, it is used to pay rent, wages, utilities, taxes, supplies and all other operating expenses. In this way, cash "flows" through a business. Cash flow is the pattern of income and expenditures and the resulting availability of cash. This idea of the *availability* of cash is important to understand. It is important because, like blood in our bodies, a certain amount of cash must always be *available* in a business. And, like blood, we can not run out of cash. So, how does a business owner make certain that cash is always available? The answer, once again, is planning. Remember that a good business plan includes a section on financing with projections of sales and operating expenses. It is here that the owner determines the necessary price for goods and services and calculates the related operating expenses, making sure that adequate cash is always available. Because many startup new businesses are not profitable for months or even years, the business is not able to create the cash necessary to operate. That is, the business uses up more cash than it creates from sales. In this case, the owner must cover this deficit from personal savings, from a loan, or other sources outside the business. Many times, this deficit is covered, at least in part, by the owner not taking any personal income from the business. Another frequent challenge for a new business is the cost of growth. Growing any business requires additional cash and the faster the growth, the more cash is required.

Because available cash and cash flow are essential to any business, the financial projections in your business plan must be accurate within a reasonable margin of error, say 20%. If you are comfortable that your projections provide this level of accuracy, and if you are sure that the necessary cash will be available, move ahead with your plan. Otherwise, seek advice from a Certified Public Accountant who specializes in small businesses, share your projection with a trusted business or financial consultant or go to another source such as a Small Business Development Center.

In conclusion, the simple rule is, make sure you never run out of cash.

# Other Considerations

*Overview* Owning and operating a small business requires great patience and persistence. The work is endlessly diverse because a small business owner is required to move quickly from one concern to another, to know many if not all the details of the business operation, to be the leader, the motivator, the decision maker and the final authority in all matters. To help understand and manage this formidable challenge, I provide the following series of Other Considerations. My hope is that you will have time to quickly read through these ideas, then, as the future unfolds and you are faced with specific needs, that you will come back to them for guidance and ideas.

*The Importance of Writing* In my college years, I never would have guessed that writing would be so important in business. That, no doubt, was the reason we were required to write so many papers for business courses. We were told that no one is a born writer, someone who instinctively knows how to write well. Rather, writing is an acquired skill, gained and honed only through much practice. And, because a business owner is required to write many things, it is necessary to develop this skill at writing. Business writing falls into the category of technical writing, that is, brief, clear, and precise. If you think about it, almost everything you are required to write in business falls into this category. You won't be writing short stories or a novel or a biography. You will be writing job descriptions, procedures, quality control standards, communications in the form of email messages, letters, applications and on and on. Each of these requires precision and clarity, the hallmarks of good technical writing. Fortunately, there are some useful standards that characterize solid technical business writing:

1. Brevity – Keeping it brief helps a reader get through a document quickly. When speaking, we often repeat ourselves and this tendency carries over to writing. But avoiding repetition helps maintain brevity. Get straight to the point when writing, using as few words as possible. Avoid compound sentences, jargon, abbreviations, acronyms, and anything that will slow the reader or cause confusion.
2. Clarity – Choose words carefully. Use simple words and avoid obscure ones. Write in short sentences and be careful about paragraphs, which, like sentences, should be short and cover only one topic. In each paragraph, move from the general to the specifics of your subject.
3. Precision – Brevity and clarity help create precision but review and revision are necessary to finally achieve it. The review should be proportional to the importance of the message. A quick review of email messages takes just seconds while reviewing something like

company policy statements requires more time and may even involve other people. Almost everything we write requires revision, from letters to procedures to email messages, so be sure all your writing gets a review. Writing reflects the writer, and you need to make certain that reflection is accurate. Use revision for precision.

*Dealing With Change* We know or have been told that change is inevitable. There are only two ways to deal with change. We can respond to it or we can create it. In my opinion, a small business owner should create change, be an *agent of change* as some say. I suggest that there are two general ways that a manager can be an agent of change:

1. Seek Change – A business owner should seek change and encourage employees to look for creative and positive ways to change. Watch for opportunities in industry publications and reports, keep tabs on competitors, establish relationships with regulators and government agencies, rely on industry specialists, business consultants and your accountant. Acknowledge and reward employees who suggest change. Make your business a place where changes and suggestions for change are encouraged and welcome.
2. Make Mistakes – One of my sons attended Garfield Elementary School in Boise where a large sign was painted on one of the walls in the lunchroom. It read, "Mistakes are good; they help us grow; they teach us what we need to know." A cute jingle, this statement is also deeply profound and worth contemplating. In business, I would change a few words to make the idea

more relevant: "Mistakes are good; they help us change; We have some things to rearrange." Watch for mistakes and errors because they often indicate that some adjustment is needed. Some mistakes, of course, are just human error and must be overlooked and forgiven. However, a good business manager will be sensitive and watchful for mistakes because they often reveal an opportunity to improve. One way to develop this sensitivity is to use an approach called "Management by Exception." In this approach, a manager watches business activity by personal observation, by reading production reports, listening to customers, talking with employees, questioning supervisors and so on. Most of the time, the work goes smoothly and predictably. Occasionally, an exception pops up, the production report is unusual, a customer complains, an employee takes unapproved leave, a supervisor reports a problem. These are the "exceptions" that should get the manager's attention – if the manager is receptive and sensitive. If significant, such exceptions should trigger a dispassionate review and discussion with those involved. Mistakes and exceptions often lead to improvements. Being open minded and not judgmental is the appropriate behavior to evaluate and benefit from them.

*Keeping it Simple* Timeless advice for small business is "Keep it simple." But doing this is never as easy as it sounds. Here are some ideas that may help you achieve this goal:

Share and Teach – Be open about what you know. Take pleasure in helping employees understand and share your enthusiasm

## OTHER CONSIDERATIONS

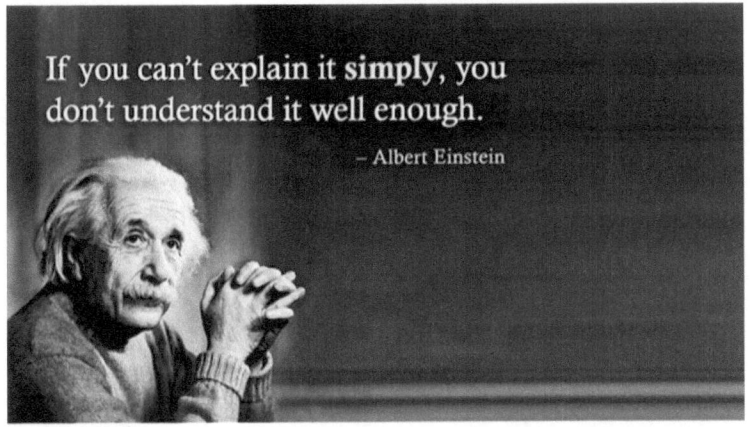

for what you do in business. Focus on one task or process at a time, emphasize essential elements, explain context and how doing top quality work has a positive impact on other people and processes.

Focus on the Customer – A sales pitch is more effective if it begins by involving the customer. Begin with broad questions like, "How can I help you?" or "Tell me about your project." As the customer responds, you can ask more detailed questions. The key here is to listen carefully and be sure to take written notes. Seek to understand the customer's needs. With this knowledge in hand, it is much easier to explain more specifically how your product or service will help.

Learn – Opportunities to improve your business surround you. Customers, employees and those who serve and supply your business will tell you what you need to know. Just ask. Follow up sales with a brief questionnaire including a few blank lines for comments and suggestions. Likewise, ask employees for feedback and ideas.

Unclutter – Clutter is distracting and distractions slow you down, divert your attention and waste time. Set an example by keeping a clean, uncluttered work area and helping others understand how important this is. Simple things like clean vehicles, clear office windows and crisp uniforms send a positive message to everyone. You care about how you look and appreciate efficient operation.

Break Down Complex Projects – Small business owners are sometimes faced with complex problems or opportunities. To control and manage complexity, break it down into the essential steps necessary to meet time and budget demands. Ask others to comment and contribute. Try to end with a one-page plan of action.

Use the Power of Three -- One example of simplicity is the use of the number three. In geometry, in architecture, and in business, three is the number to use if you can. Three of anything is easy to remember and understand. For example, the title of my book is three steps. It would be possible to come up with six or more steps for small business success, but more steps would be difficult to remember and lead a reader away from my three simple directives for business owners. If three is not enough, only add as many more as necessary; be conservative with the number. Simpler is almost always better.

Here is a personal 'keep it simple' story from early in my career in banking and finance. I was a loan officer charged with originating, or finding commercial loan opportunities. All my customers and prospects were small business owners. I met with them to explain how borrowing money from my company could help. But the process of making a loan is complex and time consuming. I was required to follow detailed procedures every step of the way, procedures spelled out in several large three ring binders that changed often with modifications from headquarters. It was impossible to know and understand all the details in those binders. While commercial lending is inherently complex and highly regulated, originating or finding a loan opportunity was fairly simple. I was caught between frustrating, intricate procedures and someone who just needed to borrow money for a specific business purpose like adding warehouse space, upgrading equipment or increasing inventory. This loan company I worked for eventually failed, in part, I believe, because of this unnecessary complexity. I often observed loan officers from other lenders making deals much faster than I could. The lesson is clear: keep it as simple as possible and always look for ways to streamline or simplify the process, especially from the customer's point of view.

*Decisions* Decision making is a vital skill for business owners. A broad range of decision types and sizes face a business owner every day. Most are small, routine, or simple decisions such as authorizing an inventory purchase, setting a delivery date, or changing a meeting time. Others are bigger decisions that may have significant consequences such as product design changes, purchasing or leasing a new computer system, or moving to another location. In almost all decisions, a manager must sort through information to determine what is relevant. For small, routine decisions, the path is usually clear because there is a routine or a protocol to be followed. Many small decisions become procedures; in other words, they become automatic. The manager needs only monitor the procedure to assure compliance.

Each decision you make has a time line attached. Complex decisions usually require more time. The general approach is to go slowly and carefully with big decisions and "don't sweat the small stuff." While most of it *is* small stuff, you occasionally are faced with a big one. Here is a checklist for making more complex decisions in small business:

1. Evaluate the Situation – Think about who, what, where, when, why will be affected by the decision. Gather information necessary to be adequately informed. Consult and seek advice from others, consider time limits, urgency, and the relative importance of the decision.
2. Analyze the Situation – Do a cost-benefit analysis to determine if the estimated costs justify the expected benefits. On one sheet of paper, list the pros and cons of the decision. Explore and consider alternatives and consult with others to see if there is consensus.
3. Apply Ethical Standards – Determine if the decision presents any ethical difficulty or conflict of interest. Make sure the decision is consistent with established business ethics and your personal and business values.
4. Develop a Back-Up Plan – If the decision fails or cannot be implemented as planned, write a brief description of "Plan B." A contingency plan can save time and money. Avoid making any big decision without a back-up plan.

*Contracts and Agreements* A small business owner is surrounded by contracts and agreements. Many are standard printed and signed documents like inventory order forms, promissory notes, leases, utility contracts and so on. Others are unique to the business-like employment agreements, work orders, service contract forms, and liability waivers. Still others may be

## OTHER CONSIDERATIONS

verbal, agreements without any written document, relying on good will and reputation. However, with very few exceptions, contracts and agreements should be in writing and signed by the individuals involved, the "parties." Here are some general guidelines on contracts and agreements for small business owners:

Timing – As with any decision, timing is a significant factor in contracts and agreements. That is, the bigger the deal, the more time it should take. Contracts and agreements almost always involve money, so it becomes an easy measure of significance; the more money involved, the bigger the deal and the more time required. This is not to say that small contracts deserve less attention. But, many small and even more significant contracts and agreements become standard forms and procedures. Examples include an employment contract, a sales agreement, a work order form, and an expense reimbursement request. These and other standard agreement forms deserve careful attention to detail and consistency. For example, all your business forms and agreements should include your logo and contact information. The same or similar wording should be used in all your contracts and agreements. This is important to establish a tone, a standard and a pattern that reflects your business culture and ethics. Once in place, all standard contract and agreement forms should be reviewed and modified annually and as needed based on feedback from employees, customers, advisors and others who may provide input and ideas for improving the forms you use.

Legality – Your contracts and agreements should be legally enforceable. However, that does not mean you need an attorney to write them. There is a better way to get this important job done. Whether you're creating a standard form or a unique contract agreement, it is wise to involve those who will be affected or obliged by them. When you do this, the document you create will be on a solid legal foundation. That is, those who are involved in the agreement and those who will be signing the contract will have helped create it. Having used this technique many times, I can recommend this simple, three-step process to any business owner:

- Step one is to make a list of the important points of agreement between the two parties to the proposed contract or agreement. Separately, the other party should do the same.
- Step two is to combine the two lists from the two parties and add narrative. Both parties should then review and agree to the final draft of the proposed contract or agreement.
- Step three is legal review if the proposed contract is sizable enough, involves a large amount of money or is otherwise significant or complex. You can ask an attorney to review and provide comment. Getting legal advice in this manner will cost much less than asking an attorney to draft the document from scratch. If the contract is small or incidental and both parties are satisfied with the content, you won't need to engage an attorney. Go ahead and print the form or contract and put it to use.

Contract Contents — There are several legal elements that should be included in any contact or agreement.

- An offer is a promise to do or provide certain things in exchange for money. For example, a small business

## OTHER CONSIDERATIONS

owner offers to wash a customer's windows or provide certain landscape services for a specific amount of money.
- Acceptance of an offer is agreement to its terms, usually by signing and dating a written document.
- Consideration is almost always a specific amount of money promised in exchange for doing or providing certain things.
- Mutuality is the shared responsibility to fulfill the terms of the agreement or contract. That is, both parties equally understand and accept the obligation to complete the transaction. For small business owners, mutuality means balance, a fair market price in exchange for certain products or services.
- Contracts and agreements should be in writing to help assure common understanding between the two parties. A verbal offer and acceptance may constitute a binding contract or agreement but are difficult to enforce if challenged.

Although contracts and agreements should almost always be in writing and signed by both parties, they are only a formality, a legal protection. Far more important is the actual performance: providing clearly superior products and services. Creating and maintaining a reputation for exceptional performance will assure success. The underlying contracts and agreements play only a supporting role in a business that earns such a reputation.

*Hiring Employees* Hiring your first employee creates a major responsibility for your business and for you personally. It is one of the biggest decisions you will face because it involves a significant amount of money and new ongoing obligations. So, following the suggestion to go slowly with such major decisions, here is a process to help you understand the issues:

Employee or Contractor? – As your business grows, you will need help keeping up with demand. A decision to hire someone raises the question of whether that person will be an employee or an independent contractor. By definition, an employee is under your control and follows your instructions and job requirements. An independent contractor is just that – independent. This person is obliged to perform certain tasks, usually under a written contract, but is not under your direct control as an employer. This is an important distinction because many small businesses get into trouble by calling people contractors when they are really employees. If in doubt, you can contact your local department of labor office for advice.

Job Description – The first step when hiring your first employee is to write a job description. The appendix of this book includes a one-page sample format you can use. Writing a job description requires you to consider exactly what the employee will be required to do and what experience and skills are necessary. It is a useful tool you can use when interviewing and selecting an employee and later, reviewing job performance and planning for the future with that employee.

Employee Handbook – Before hiring your first employee, it may be wise to consider creating an employee handbook. Such a handbook compels the business owner to think about policies and procedures in a number of areas of the business such as employment policies, hours of work, compensation and payroll practices, standards of conduct, employee performance, employment benefits, time off and absences. Fortunately, there are many free or low-cost examples of employee handbooks available on the internet. Another source of assistance may be your local college or university where business students can be engaged for course credit to help write a handbook just for you. Keep in mind that an employee handbook will need revision and updating from time to time in response to changes in the business. For example, a growing business will probably need to adjust its compensation program to allow for more categories, pay scales, and benefits. Although challenging to create, an employee handbook will become a valuable and indispensable management tool.

Labor Laws – Each state and the federal government have many laws governing employment and labor. Most of these laws have been in place for many years and have changed and evolved through the legal system. To be safe and assure compliance, visit your local department of labor office. While you don't need to know everything about all the laws, it is wise to be aware of your responsibilities under the law as an employer.

Hiring Report – Within a short period of time after hiring an employee, usually 20 days or so, an employer must inform the state department of labor office of the hire. This is required so that the labor office can compile labor statistics and communicate with you as a new employer.

Income Tax Withholding – An employer is required to withhold federal income tax from an employee's salary or wages. In addition, states that have an income tax also require withholding. The amounts withheld are calculated based on formulas and schedules provided by the Internal Revenue Service and the individual state tax commission. These amounts are then reported to the taxing office at the end of each month or calendar quarter and the actual dollars withheld are deposited into tax accounts controlled by them. Much, if not all this record keeping, reporting, and depositing can be done electronically through on-line websites.

Social Security and Medicare Withholding – Employers are required to withhold and pay these federal taxes. An employer is responsible to pay half of both of these taxes. The record keeping and payment requirements are combined with the federal income tax reporting system.

Unemployment Insurance – Every employer is obliged to pay all of an employee's unemployment insurance. This insurance is designed to protect employees who become unemployed. For example, if a business fails, its employees should be eligible to collect a modest income from the insurance fund until new employment can be found. The same is true if an employee is terminated. On the other hand, if an employee quits, the insurance may not be available. It is up to the employee to apply for compensation from the unemployment insurance fund. The cost of unemployment insurance varies from time to time based on the overall activity of the insurance fund and of the individual employer. Once again, the employer is required to keep certain employment records and report and pay regularly into the unemployment insurance fund. The state department of labor administers the unemployment insurance fund.

Workers' Compensation Insurance – This protects employees who suffer a job-related injury or disease. The employer is required to pay the full insurance premium. Like unemployment insurance, workers' compensation laws require certain

## OTHER CONSIDERATIONS

record keeping, reporting and premium payments. A separate state agency usually administers the workers' compensation laws but the actual insurance is available through the agency, a private insurance provider or, in some cases, a large employer may be self-insured.

Other Requirements — Every state has unique requirements related to employment. For example, Idaho, like many states, imposes a tax on business equipment and facilities that requires the owner to file an annual report and pay an appropriate tax. If the business owns real estate, it is required to pay local real estate taxes. Vehicles used in the business come with license and registration taxes. On the federal level, businesses with more than five employees must comply with laws governing human rights such as the Americans with Disabilities Act, non-discrimination laws, fair labor standards laws and regulations and others.

# Appendix and Additional Resources

*Overview* This final section of my book includes guidelines, samples and examples of different aspects of starting, owning and operating a small business. It is a compilation of the helpful resources I have accumulated over a period of many decades when I was a lender, an educator, a counselor and a small business owner. With one exception, all of these resources are tried and true, having been used, revised, and improved over time. The one exception is the last on the list, the B Corporation movement which appeals to my sense of social justice and personal accountability in business. I believe this idea has great promise for linking business to unmet social needs in our country and around the world. See for yourself if the B Corporation idea is appropriate for you. As always, however, I begin with planning, the essential foundation for any business.

*Business Planning Guide* Many years ago, I was employed by Boise State University here in Idaho to do two things. First, I was given the opportunity to counsel and assist owners and entrepreneurs in a new university program sponsored by the U.S. Small Business Administration. The idea behind the program was to make the resources of the university available to the small business community. My other responsibility was to teach in collaboration with two other members of the department of management in the College of Business at BSU. As it turned out, business planning was a central concern and need for both efforts. Helping small business owners and entrepreneurs develop and refine a plan became our principal service. We provided research information, helped develop ideas and strategies, calculated financial projections and even assisted with writing. The end result was a written business plan. In many cases, the plan was not finished or implemented because it was faulty in some way. Often, the background research did not support the business idea. In other cases, the financial requirements could not be met or the owner abandoned the effort. In a few instances, however, the business owners went on to create or grow successful businesses. Many of these success stories continue to thrive today in the Boise area.

In the classroom, usually filled with aspiring entrepreneurs, the concept of business planning also applied. Here, the semester assignment was to create a business plan for an enterprise the student wanted to create. Along the way, we interviewed eight or ten small business owners in our evening classes. These owners were invited from a list of prospects provided by the students who always knew someone who owned a small business or wanted to know more about a local small business. Over a period of nine years while I was in this teaching position at BSU, I don't recall ever being turned down by a business owner. Each one I invited to class was pleased by the invitation and eager to share their experience. This live conversation between business owners and students was a highly effective learning method and often dramatic when owners shared stories of risk, struggle, failure, and success. At the end of the semester, each student submitted a written business plan which I carefully read and provided my opinion. What follows is the business planning guide I used back then with some recent modifications and minor improvements.

## Business Planning Guide

*Summary*

On one page, write an overview of the business, its definition and purpose and the industry in which it operates. Describe how you will operate and manage it and state your motivation and goals. (It will be easier to write this summary after the rest of the business plan is finished.)

*The Business and the Industry*

In more detail, define the business and describe your objective or mission for the business. Outline the general strategy you will follow. Tell how the business is organized and who owns it. Describe important facilities and other necessary resources. Summarize any unique or special competencies and proprietary resources. Describe the industry in which the business operates starting with the big national picture and narrowing the focus to the local market. Include information on trends, segments, cycles, problems, and opportunities in the industry. List important trade associations, publications, laws, and regulations.

## Marketing Plan

Describe the local market in which the business operates, its size in dollars, units, and segments. Include information about competitors. Describe the products and services of the business. List key aspects, features, and issues of the market and identify specific problems and opportunities. Summarize information from market studies and research. State the marketing strategy. List sales and promotion goals and the criteria used to measure success. Calculate a marketing budget.

## Financial Plan

Prepare projected income statements and balance sheets for five years. Calculate the break-even point and unit cost. Estimate startup and expansion costs. Relate the projections to industry standards and ratios. List quantitative criteria used to measure the success of the financial plan.

## Operations Plan

Summarize the manufacturing or service delivery process. Consider production and operations schedules, raw materials and finished goods inventory and controls. List sources of supply and services. Describe the quality control system, labor and training requirements, support services and facilities, seasonal needs, utility, mechanical and other essential operating requirements.

## Management Plan

Explain how the business will be run and by whom. Write a brief resume for the person in charge, listing knowledge, skill, experience, training, and certification. Describe the management style, methods, and techniques. Define a code of business ethics to be used.

*Other Considerations*

Describe unique or distinctive aspects of the business such as weather and climate, transportation and support requirements of location, financial sources, personal experience, succession issues, relations with relatives and investors, timing, licensing, regulatory requirements, emerging opportunities, and so on.

*Supporting Documents*

Assemble and organize the important research and industry documents used to write and support the plan. Include spreadsheets, resumes, personal financial statements, tax returns, industry and marketing studies, survey results, letters of intent and support, organizational documents, agreements, photographs, diagrams, job descriptions, technical drawings, blueprints, operations and technical manuals, product information sheets, price lists and similar documents and information that support and embellish the business plan.

*Sample Job Description* Written job descriptions have several important uses for small businesses. They make you consider exactly what an employee will be required to do and what experience and skills are necessary. It is a useful tool you can use when interviewing and selecting employees and later, reviewing job performance and planning for the future with that employee. From the employee's perspective, a job description provides performance guidelines and expectations. In addition, carefully written job descriptions for each position in the business are the building blocks of an organization.

In an organizational chart, they show the structure of the business and the lines of authority. They are also helpful when it comes to developing a compensation plan for the business. Having the job description allows you to compare your job with identical or similar jobs in your county and state. Compensation surveys are one way to make this comparison. This survey information is available from the state's department of labor and from trade associations, and human resource consultants and organizations. You can also do your own research by questioning others in similar businesses. Competition for qualified job applicants and stable, experienced employees can be fierce. Knowing the going wage or salary for jobs you will be offering can help you select and keep talented employees. It all begins with an accurate and regularly updated job description.

Following is a general job description format. Adapt this to your unique business and use a similar format for all positions. Because your business exists in a dynamic environment, change is inevitable. Review each job description with the incumbent and update all your job descriptions and compensation plan once each year.

## Job Description Format

**Job Title** Landscape Maintenance Crew Supervisor

**General Description** This is an official position with broad responsibility for training, supervising, and managing landscape maintenance crew functions. Reporting is to the President.

## Principal Duties

- Train and supervise landscape maintenance crew members
- Monitor crew performance on the work site
- Schedule and oversee equipment maintenance
- Maintain and provide work performance records and reports
- Seek and suggest ways to improve crew training, procedures, and efficiency
- Act as the communication link between the business and customers
- Report and collaborate closely with the President
- Perform related work as requested

## Desirable Knowledge, Skill and Experience

- Knowledge and skill in operating and maintaining landscape maintenance equipment
- At least two years' experience as a crew supervisor in a landscape or similar business
- Work experience as a customer service representative, dealing directly with customers
- Skill in evaluating performance and maintenance of landscape maintenance equipment
- Any equivalent combination of knowledge, skill, and experience.

**Other Position Requirements** The Landscape Maintenance Crew Supervisor is, by definition, a specialist in, is responsible for, and is knowledgeable about the work of a landscape maintenance crew and the equipment used.

The supervisor is expected to provide regular reporting and discussion of crew and equipment performance to the president. In addition, the supervisor is the primary, on-going communication link with customers to assure their satisfaction and continuation of service.

*The Small Business Checkup* How healthy is your business? Like personal health, an annual health checkup can provide valuable information and ideas for improving the overall well-being and stability of your business. Following is a self-guided review of the major elements of business: marketing, operations, finance, management and other considerations. Use this checklist to identify areas in your business that need attention or adjustment. You can also use the checkup to find opportunities, clarify challenges and generally improve business performance. I suggest doing this once each year as part of the annual review and update of your business plan.

Step 1. Marketing: Know and Serve your Market

- ❐ Review the description of the market you serve.
- ❐ Is the dollar size of your market growing or shrinking?
- ❐ Have the geographic boundaries of the market changed?
- ❐ Does the market have new or changed segments or divisions?
- ❐ Update your list of competitors, their strengths and weaknesses.
- ❐ Are you in regular contact and communication with customers?
- ❐ Are there any new or significant factors that influence the market?

## Step 2. Operations: Review and Evaluate your Operation

- ❐ How has your manufacturing or service delivery process changed?
- ❐ Review your production cycle or sequence of operation
- ❐ Are new knowledge, skills, and abilities needed in your business?
- ❐ Examine and evaluate production equipment and facilities
- ❐ Study your list of key suppliers and vendors. Are new players in the market?
- ❐ Calculate the current unit cost of production
- ❐ Evaluate seasonal and periodic variables
- ❐ Review and evaluate your quality control process

## Step 3. Finance: How the money flows through the business

- ❐ Update your financial forecast of revenue and expense
- ❐ Study and adjust your balance sheet
- ❐ Recompute your break-even point
- ❐ Research industry financial ratios and standards
- ❐ Review and evaluate financial recordkeeping and reporting routines

## Step 4. Management: How the business is run

- ❐ Examine your organizational chart
- ❐ Are all job titles with salaries and wages listed?
- ❐ Review job descriptions and plan performance reviews
- ❐ Review the management philosophy and the management cycle
- ❐ Update management reports and schedules

- ☐ Review forms, checklists and manuals used in the business
- ☐ Update contact information for key suppliers, vendors and professionals

Step 5. Other Considerations: Additional factors affecting business

- ☐ Review the long-term goal for the business
- ☐ Do you need a succession plan?
- ☐ Check your business organizational documents
- ☐ Review contractual agreements
- ☐ Update the business plan
- ☐ Update the list of proprietary assets and their value
- ☐ Update your personal financial statement

*Creating a Company Newsletter* A newsletter can be a good vehicle to stay in contact with those people and groups that are important to the business, customers, vendors, suppliers and consultants, investors, lenders and employees. It is a way to promote your company name and reinforce your identity. It offers an opportunity to reflect an attitude and a level of excellence you want to achieve. It is a way to keep people informed and involved and to recognize their individual importance to the business. There are many questions regarding business newsletters, like what information should go into it? Does a newsletter give an advantage to a competitor by disclosing information about your business? How often should you publish your newsletter? What is the best format for a newsletter, printed, email, or social media? The options are endless and so are the questions.

After numerous years writing newsletters in my own business, I learned many things about them which I am pleased to share here. First, allow me to review the basics of newsletters, the tried and true guidelines for producing almost any newsletter.

Create an Identity – Start a newsletter by creating a permanent masthead, your unique design. Use your logo, your byline and your color scheme and stick with it. In time, you will create an identity that people will recognize and remember with good feelings. You want to capture attention instantly by having a clear and quick identity.

Keep it Brief – Today, everyone with a smartphone, a tablet or a desktop computer is subject to a daily barrage of information. In addition, most of our daily mail is junk and quickly discarded. To get read, a newsletter must be brief and quickly read, two pages maximum. Use simple words, short sentences and paragraphs. Avoid exclamation marks and stick to simple facts without embellishment. Understatement is best and appreciated.

Focus on Support – In addition to some important news like a milestone achieved or a goal met, a newsletter should offer assistance and support. Tell the reader how you provide these and how to get them. Strive to create good will and helpfulness.

Give Contact Information – At the end of the newsletter, always include full contact information so readers can quickly and easily respond using the medium they prefer.

*Sample Profit Sharing Program* One of the most powerful motivators for employees is a cash profit sharing program.

This simple practice is just right for small businesses. Unlike other employee benefit options like retirement plans, profit sharing has no significant administrative cost and it is flexible. That is, the amount of profit sharing will change depending on the amount of profit generated by the business and how much of it the owner decides to share. Following is an example of a typical profit-sharing program. Let's use the example from above for a company with a $45,000 net profit for the year.

| Profit Distribution  Sample Company with $45,000 net profit | | |
| --- | --- | --- |
| | $ | % |
| Profit Sharing | 22,500 | 50% |
| Management Bonuses | 9,000 | 20% |
| Retained Earnings | 6,750 | 15% |
| Equipment Upgrades | 4,500 | 10% |
| Other Uses | 2,250 | 5% |
| Totals | 45,000 | 100% |

In this example, the business owner has decided to share $22,500 of the net profit with employees. Assume that the business has five employees including the owner. Each employee gets ten points for each year or fraction with the company and one point for each $1,000 of annual income from salaries or wages. Here is a worksheet that shows the details of this point system.

## Sample Cash Profit Sharing Worksheet

| Employees | Annual Wages | Wage Points (wages ÷ 1,000) | Years of Employment (rounded up) | Employment Points (years X 10) | Total Points | Profit Sharing for Each Point ($22,500 ÷ 210) | Individual Share of Profit |
|---|---|---|---|---|---|---|---|
| Mary | $25,000 | 25 | 4 | 40 | 65 | $107.14 | $6,964 |
| Joseph | $23,000 | 23 | 3 | 30 | 53 | $107.14 | $5,679 |
| Art | $18,000 | 18 | 2 | 20 | 38 | $107.14 | $4,071 |
| Jennifer | $18,000 | 18 | 1 | 10 | 28 | $107.14 | $3,000 |
| William | $16,000 | 16 | 1 | 10 | 26 | $107.14 | $2,786 |
| Totals | $100,000 | 100 | 11 | 110 | 210 | $107.14 | $22,500 |

Notice that this point system emphasizes years of employment with the business. This is a way of encouraging employees to stay because profit sharing increases significantly with each additional year of employment. To make this approach even more motivational, the owner could give ten points for each six months of employment rather than each year.

Profit-sharing distribution is like any other employee compensation. That is, profit sharing is subject to income tax withholding and all other standard deductions and charges. This way, the employee is not required to consider additional tax consequences when filing a tax return. All of the employee tax information including profit sharing is provided in each employee's annual W2 Wage and Tax Statement.

When presenting the profit-sharing distribution, the business owner may want to write an individual note, something like this:

## MEMO

To:        Jennifer Porter
Date:      Thursday, January 10, 2019
Regarding: 2018 Profit Sharing

I am pleased to present your 2018 profit sharing check for $3,000 along with my sincere thanks for helping make the year successful in so many ways.

Your share of our net profit is based on a point system, one point for each $1,000 of compensation received during the year and ten points for each year or fraction of employment with the company.

You'll notice that your check is dated December 31, 2018. We did this so that the tax withholding would be reflected in the 2018 records including your W-2 Wage and Tax Statement mailed to you earlier this month.

Congratulations, Jennifer.

*Developing a Financial Projection* You may need an accountant to help with this task. However, if you know how to manipulate a computer spreadsheet, it is not difficult. You will recall that a financial projection is required as part of your business plan. The idea is to forecast five or more years into the future so you can anticipate and plan for growth in income, expenses, and net profit. The way to start this is with a carefully developed budget for the coming year. In the following example, that

# APPENDIX AND ADDITIONAL RESOURCES

year is 2019. The business in this example is a small landscape maintenance company.

Based on the projected income and expenses for 2019, the owner anticipates growth in income at 20% per year, a reasonable expectation in a good market. Expenses are forecast to grow at about 15% per year.

| Sample Projected Financial Statements for 2019 through 2023 | | | | | | |
|---|---|---|---|---|---|---|
| | 2019 Budget | | 2020 | 2021 | 2022 | 2023 |
| | $ | % | $ | $ | $ | $ |
| **Income** | | | | | | |
| Maintenance Fee Income | 150,000 | 81% | 180,000 | 216,000 | 260,000 | 312,000 |
| Product Sales Income | 35,000 | 19% | 42,000 | 50,000 | 60,000 | 72,000 |
| Total Income | 185,000 | 100% | 222,000 | 266,000 | 320,000 | 384,000 |
| **Expenses** | | | | | | |
| Salaries & Wages | 100,000 | 71% | 115,000 | 132,000 | 152,000 | 180,000 |
| Employment Taxes | 9,000 | 6% | 10,400 | 12,000 | 14,400 | 16,000 |
| Equipment Lease | 4,000 | 3% | 4,600 | 5,400 | 6,200 | 7,000 |
| Supplies | 13,000 | 9% | 15,000 | 17,000 | 20,000 | 23,000 |
| Utilities, Phone & Internet | 3,000 | 2% | 3,500 | 4,000 | 4,600 | 6,000 |
| Insurance | 2,000 | 1% | 2,300 | 2,700 | 3,100 | 4,000 |
| Promotion | 1,000 | 1% | 1,100 | 1,400 | 1,600 | 2,000 |
| Equipment Repair & Maint. | 5,000 | 4% | 5,700 | 6,500 | 7,500 | 9,000 |
| Capital Reserve | 2,000 | 1% | 2,300 | 2,700 | 3,100 | 4,000 |
| Miscellaneous | 1,000 | 1% | 1,100 | 1,300 | 1,500 | 2,000 |
| Total Expenses | 140,000 | 100% | 161,000 | 185,000 | 214,000 | 253,000 |
| Net Income | 45,000 | | 61,000 | 81,000 | 106,000 | 131,000 |
| Net Profit % | 24% | | 27% | 30% | 33% | 34% |
| (Net Profit % = Net Income ÷ Total Income) | | | | | | |

Even though all these numbers are estimates, they do provide a framework for making decisions as the year progresses. They also provide a number of financial goals. For example, the business owner will attempt to contract for landscape maintenance with enough homeowners to generate the income goal of $185,000 in 2019. This number can be broken down into how many landscape contracts are needed to reach this number. Say a typical contract for a residential home landscape maintenance is $300 per month for eight months each year. That equals $2,400 for the average contract ($300 per month x 8 months). If this is the average contract amount, the owner will need to generate about 75 contracts for the year (total income of $185,000 ÷ $2,400 per contract). This, then, is the contract goal for the year – 75 contracts.

A financial projection also provides a framework for monitoring expenses. Actual expenses can be compared with the projected expenses. To do this, the business owner will need a breakdown by month during the operating year. For landscape maintenance companies, this presents a challenge because during the three or four months of winter, little or no income is being generated and expenses should also go way down.

Financial projections are useful and necessary for a small business. As time goes by and actual numbers are reported on financial statements, accuracy of the projections will improve. What's important is to take the time to make the projections in the first place and update them annually as results come in. That way, the business owner always has a five-year projection into the future.

*The B Corporation Concept* The June 2016 issue of the Harvard Business Review includes an article by Suntae Kin, Matthew J. Karlesky, Christopher G. Myers and Todd Schifeling. The title of the article is *Why Companies are Becoming B Corporations*. In it, the authors explain the nature and purpose of B Corporations:

"Certified B Corporations are social enterprises verified by B Lab, a nonprofit organization. B Lab certifies companies based on how they create value for non-shareholding stakeholders, such as their employees, the local community, and the environment. Once a firm crosses a certain performance threshold on these dimensions, it makes amendments to its corporate charter to incorporate the interests of all stakeholders into the fiduciary duties of directors and officers. These steps demonstrate that a firm is following a fundamentally different governance philosophy than a traditional shareholder-centered corporation.

The first generation of B Corporations was certified in 2007, and the number of firms earning certification has grown exponentially ever since. Today, there are more than 1,700 B Corporations in 50 countries. Although any company, regardless of its size, legal structure, or industry, can become a B Corporation, currently most B Corporations are privately-held small and medium-sized businesses."

While the total number of certified B corporations is relatively small, it continues to grow and now includes Ben and Jerry's, the ice cream maker and Patagonia, the outdoor sports equipment and clothing retailer. In addition to altruistic motivations, these companies see the B corporation concept as a way to influence customers in a positive way. In its decision making, the B corporation includes factors involving the various environments in which it operates. For example, it takes into consideration the needs, the health and the long-term security of employees. It includes factors such as income inequality, sustainability, the mission and the ethics that guide the business.

Learn more at the website bcorporation.net.

www.ingramcontent.com/pod-product-compliance
Lightning Source LLC
Chambersburg PA
CBHW030455220526
45464CB00006B/2544